PALOMINO HORSES

AUSTRIA'S HAFLINGERS

For a free color catalog describing Gareth Stevens' list of high-quality books, call 1-800-542-2595 (USA) or
1-800-461-9120 (Canada). Gareth Stevens' Fax: (414) 225-0377.

Library of Congress Cataloging-in-Publication Data available upon request from publisher.
Fax: (414) 225-0377 for the attention of the Publishing Records Department.

ISBN 0-8368-1369-3

This edition first published in North America in 1995 by
Gareth Stevens Publishing
1555 North RiverCenter Drive, Suite 201
Milwaukee, Wisconsin 53212, USA

First published in Great Britain in 1994 by Sunburst Books, Deacon House, 65 Old Church Street, London, SW3 5BS.
Photographs © 1989 Franckh'sche Verlagshandlung, W. Keller & Co., Stuttgart, Germany. Text © 1994 Sunburst Books.
Additional end matter © 1995 by Gareth Stevens, Inc.

U.S. Series Editor: Patricia Lantier-Sampon
U.S. Editor: Barbara J. Behm

Printed in China

1 2 3 4 5 6 7 8 9 9 99 98 97 96 95

MAGNIFICENT HORSES OF THE WORLD

PALOMINO HORSES
AUSTRIA'S HAFLINGERS

Photography by
Tomáš Míček
Elisabeth Kellner

Text by
Dr. Hans-Jörg Schrenk

Gareth Stevens Publishing
MILWAUKEE

A herd of young Haflinger stallions. At one time, this horse was bred only in a region of Austria known as the Tyrol. Today, Haflingers are found worldwide.

Preceding pages: In Austria, Haflingers spend their summers high in the mountains. They live there for months without any human contact.

The Haflinger is a small, good-natured horse, perfect for riding. It is chestnut in color with a white mane. This type of coloring is called "palomino." The Haflinger is descended from the Arabian thoroughbred.

Stallions spend most of the warmer summer months in mountain
pastures until the age of two. In these wild areas, they can
grow as nature intended, becoming healthy and strong.
The young stallions play-fight with one another.
This establishes a hierarchy within the herd.

The ideal stallion has an elegant head and a long, flowing mane.
Its chestnut coloring has white points.

Written records dating back to the Middle Ages describe small, tough mountain horses living in the Southern Alps, part of a European mountain range. These horses were used to pull wagons and carry heavy loads on their backs to isolated villages and farms of the mountain communities. They could easily climb steep, narrow mountain paths with their small, sure hooves.

Haflingers are the result of crossbreeding these native horses with Arabian thoroughbreds. The Arabian horses were brought to the area, which is now Austria, as a result of the Crusades and wars against the Turks.

The birth of the official Haflinger breed was declared in 1874. In 1904, the first Haflinger breeders' association was formed. The purpose of this organization is to improve the breed. Over time, a horse with a greater variety of uses has developed. Today, Haflingers are used for riding, pulling wagons, and in farming.

Although, in recent times, there has been a decrease in the number of horses throughout Europe, the Haflinger continues to win fans worldwide. There are now over 100,000 Haflingers in existence.

The Haflinger is a lively horse that often moves in bursts of wild leaps and gallops.

Today, the main Haflinger breeding area in Austria is in the northern Tyrol. Breeding programs have taken place there since 1900.

The ideal height of the Haflinger is 54-58 inches (137-147 centimeters) for mares; 56-59 inches (142-150 cm) for stallions.

The Haflinger is bred to be a square, stocky horse. Its legs are well muscled.

Two young stallions groom each other. Usually, two horses that are friendly with one another help take care of each other's skin. Each nibbles at the skin on the neck and back of the other in hard-to-reach places. This rids the horses of troublesome insects and, in the spring, an itchy winter coat.

It is difficult for mares and foals to find food on the bare mountainsides. It often snows heavily in the mountains, even in the middle of summer. The horses must search for food beneath the snow.

Food in the mountain pastures is scarce but nourishing to the horses.
The grasses and herbs contain large amounts of minerals
that help foals grow strong. Foals drink mother's
milk for the first six months of life.

Curious horses peer at the photographer. Haflingers only rarely see people in the mountain environment of Austria.

Haflinger foals are usually born outdoors, in mountain pastures. No human help or interference takes place. This newborn is being licked dry by its mother.

Foals are able to follow their mothers everywhere just a few hours after they are born. This four-week-old already strays quite far from its mother. The foal is curious to discover everything about its mountain home.

Through crossbreeding with Arabian thoroughbreds, Haflingers were transformed from packhorses into lighter horses more suitable for riding. Since 1976, however, this particular form of crossbreeding has fallen out of favor.

This young filly, standing next to her mother, is only a few weeks old.

Haflingers roll on the ground (above) to remove extra or tangled hair and to scratch their backs.

The stallion pictured on the left feels threatened by another stallion moving in on his territory.

The unmistakable features of a Haflinger include a white, flowing mane; small ears; and a smooth, powerful croup.

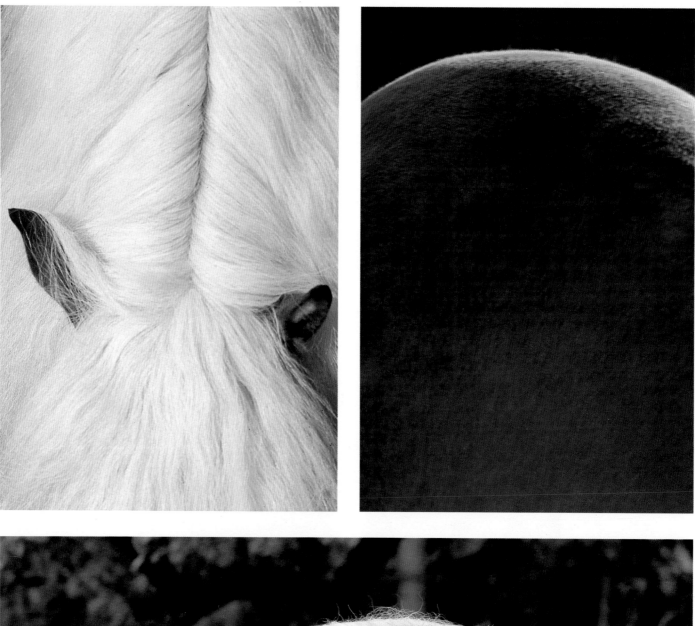

Horses are often bothered by flying insects.

A Haflinger stallion grazes on the wild grasses of a mountain pasture. Haflingers also eat hay, vegetables, grains, and tree bark.

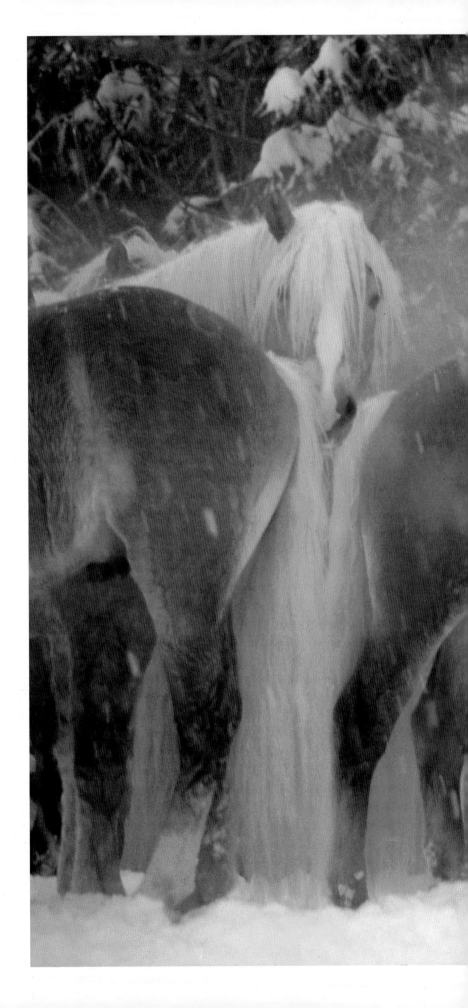

Haflingers can withstand heavy snow and bitter cold. Because of the harsh mountain environment in Austria, Haflingers become very tough and develop an excellent constitution.

Haflingers are uniform in their coloring and markings. Several individuals can work well together as a team. This is important when the horses are put to work pulling a carriage or in farming.

Haflingers sometimes keep warm in winter by participating in play-fights and other games.

At the beginning of the twentieth century, Haflingers were limited to the Tyrol. Since 1945, this small, strong breed has become more widely known. The horses are now popular in Europe, the United States, Australia, Africa, and Asia.

Haflingers are regarded as particularly important in Asia, where their genes are improving the native packhorse breeds.

Haflingers are hard-working, adaptable, strong, and long lived. Because of their healthy mountain upbringing, these horses are often able to work until they are forty years old.

From a tiny corner of the Alps, these magnificent horses have won the hearts of the entire world.

In their mountain home, Haflingers run in herds.

The clear eyes and fine head of an impressive Haflinger stallion.

Haflingers stay in peak condition by galloping with the herd.

In the Tyrol, Haflingers are raised naturally, far from the hectic modern world.

Glossary

breed — animals having specific traits; to produce offspring.

chestnut — reddish brown in color.

constitution — personality type or temperament.

crossbreeding — mating a male of one breed with a female of another.

croup — the rump of a four-legged animal.

filly — a young female horse.

foals — newborn male or female horses.

gallop — a fast way of running by an animal, such as a horse.

herd — a number of animals of one kind that stay together and travel as a group.

hierarchy — the ranking of individuals within a group from the most powerful to the least powerful.

mane — the long hair around the neck of a horse.

mares — female horses.

stallion — a mature male horse used for breeding.

thoroughbred — a horse or other animal that is bred from the best blood through a long line.

More Books About Horses

Album of Horses. Marguerite Henry (Macmillan)
America's Horses and Ponies. Irene Brady (Houghton Mifflin)
Complete Book of Horses and Horsemanship. C. W. Anderson (Macmillan)
Guide to the Horses of the World. Caroline Silver (Exeter)
Horse Breeds and Breeding. Jane Kidd (Crescent)
Horse Happy: A Complete Guide to Owning Your Own Horse. Barbara J. Berry (Bobbs-Merrill)
The Horse and Pony Manual. David Hunt (Chartwell)
Horses and Riding. George Henschel (Franklin Watts)
The New Complete Book of the Horse. Jane Holderness-Roddam (Smithmark)
The Ultimate Horse Book. Elwyn Hartley Edwards (Dorling Kindersley)
The Whole Horse Catalog. Steven D. Price, editor (Simon and Schuster)
Wild and Wonderful Horses. Cristopher Brown, ed. (Antioch)

Videos

The Art of Riding Series. (Visual Education Productions)
The Horse Family. (International Film Bureau)
Horses! (Encyclopedia Britannica)
The Mare and Foal. (Discovery Trail)
Nature: Wild Horses. (Warner Home Video)

PLACES TO WRITE

Here are some places to write for more information about horses. When you write, include your name and address, and be specific about the information you would like to receive. Don't forget to enclose a stamped, self-addressed envelope for a reply.

National Association for Humane
   and Environmental Education
P.O. Box 362
East Haddam, CT 06423-0362

Horse Council of British Columbia
5746B 176A Street
Cloverdale, British Columbia
V3S 4C7

Pennsylvania Horsebreeder's
   Association
701 East Baltimore Pike, Suite C1
Kennett Square, PA 19348

INDEX